ISSUES AND ANSWERS *Collection*

HEROES & HERETICS

Solving the Modern Mystery of the Ancient Church

MICHAEL J. SVIGEL

FOREWORD BY CHARLES R. SWINDOLL

INSIGHT FOR LIVING

HEROES AND HERETICS
Solving the Modern Mystery of the Ancient Church

By Michael J. Svigel, Th.M., Ph.D. candidate, Dallas Theological Seminary

Editor in Chief: Cynthia Swindoll, President, Insight for Living
Vice President: Wayne Stiles, Th.M., D.Min., Dallas Theological Seminary
Content Editors: Melissa Carlisle, M.A., Christian Education, Dallas Theological Seminary
        Brie Engeler, B.A., University Scholars, Baylor University
Copy Editor: Jim Craft, M.A., English, Mississippi College
Proofreaders: Maridee Dietzel, B.A., Communications/Print Media, Moody Bible Institute
        Mike Penn, B.A., Journalism, University of Oklahoma
Cover Designer: Libby Nicholson, B.F.A., Communication Graphics, Texas Christian University
Production Artist: Nancy Gustine, B.F.A., Advertising Art, University of North Texas
Cover Images: www.photos.com

Published by IFL Publishing House, A Division of Insight for Living
Post Office Box 251007, Plano, Texas 75025-1007

Scripture quotations are from the *New American Standard Bible®* (NASB). Copyright © 1960, 1962, 1963, 1968, 1971, 1972, 1973, 1975, 1977, 1995 by The Lockman Foundation. All rights reserved. Used by permission. (www.Lockman.org)

An effort has been made to locate sources and obtain permission where necessary for the quotations used in this book. In the event of any unintentional omission, a modification will gladly be incorporated in future printings.

ISBN 1-57972-705-0

Printed in the United States of America

Table of Contents

Foreword

Each fall young Christian men and women enroll in secular colleges and universities, stepping boldly out of the security of Bible-believing churches into a virtual lion's den of vicious attacks on their faith. Some survive and thrive. But to the shock of parents and pastors, many come home with new theories about the Bible's origin, the "historical Jesus," and ancient alternatives to biblical Christianity. And because these attacks target the *history* of the Bible and the church, many biblically astute pastors won't be equipped to respond.

In fact, some of the most mature, Bible-believing Christians don't know much about what happened to the church after the apostle John lifted his pen from the last word of Revelation. To many, the truth about the ancient church is a modern mystery. They would have a hard time answering critical questions like:

- How did the earliest Christians preserve the truth before the writings of the apostles were gathered into a single book called the *New Testament*?

- How do we know the early Christians didn't tamper with Scripture or change their beliefs about Jesus?

- Is the biblical faith we believe today the same faith as Christians held in the second generation?

For most Christians, a dark abyss of ignorance spans the time from the apostles to the period of the Reformation. And in recent decades unbelievers have been filling this gap with "alternative" histories of the church. The far-fetched conspiracy of *The Da Vinci Code* is but one extreme version. Chances are, you've seen some of the more respectable and persuasive experts on television specials about Jesus or the Bible.

Let me be frank. While unbelievers have been filling the abyss with revised history and bad theology, most Bible-believing Christians have been ignoring it. "After all," some feel, "because we have the Bible, why should we care about church history?"

Insight for Living has always been committed to communicating the truths of Scripture and the person of Jesus Christ in an accurate, clear, and practical manner. Today, the attacks on the origins of Scripture and the history of the church call us to step up to the plate and meet these historical challenges head-on.

This unique guide, *Heroes and Heretics: Solving the Modern Mystery of the Ancient Church*, offers you a crash course in the earliest and most crucial years of the church—those of its formation. Believe me, there's a lot more that could be said than what this short guide covers, but we've narrowed it down to a few key areas: Jesus Christ, Scripture, and the tradition of orthodoxy.

Equipping believers . . . answering critics . . . filling the gap. My prayer is that this resource will help you discover what every believer should know about the early church . . . and why.

Chuck Swindoll

Charles R. Swindoll

About the Author

Michael J. Svigel received his B.S. in Bible from Philadelphia Biblical University and his Th.M. in New Testament from Dallas Theological Seminary, where he is currently completing his Ph.D. in Historical Theology. Besides writing full-time for Insight for Living, Michael regularly teaches and speaks on a variety of biblical, theological, and historical issues. He also writes articles for academic and popular audiences as well as several types of fiction. He resides in the Dallas area with his wife Stephanie and their children.

The Fish

Notice the fish symbol on the cover of this book. Today you can find it on everything from bumpers to Bibles. Aside from the cross, the fish may be the most recognizable icon of Christianity. Yet many do not realize that the contemporary symbol of the fish is also one of the most ancient. The symbol dates back to the second century AD, appearing in the artwork of the catacombs, where Christians often gathered to avoid their Roman persecutors.

Like today's Christians, early believers used the symbol to proclaim their faith. But to the Greek-speaking Christians, the fish encapsulated the very heart of the Christian message. The Greek word for "fish," *ichthus*, formed an acrostic in which the letters stood for an early confession: "Jesus Christ, Son of God, Savior."

Ιησους	(*I*esous)	Jesus
Χριστος	(*Ch*ristos)	Christ
Θεου	(*Th*eou)	of God
Υιος	(*U*ios)	Son
Σωτηρ	(*S*oter)	Savior

When we display the fish symbol today, we not only proclaim our belief in Jesus Christ as the Son of God and Savior, but we also connect with the heroes of old who gave their lives in the face of heretics who denied Him.

ISSUES AND ANSWERS *Collection*

HEROES &
HERETICS

Solving the Modern Mystery of the Ancient Church

Heroes and Heretics:
Solving the Modern Mystery of the Ancient Church

Yawn . . . history class . . . again. . . .

A stiff, wooden chair, stale air, and a ten-year-old textbook that looks like it's never been read. A teacher drones on and on about people and places you care nothing about. Finally the bell rings, waking you from your stupor, and you escape to the fresh air of reality—the here and now of real life.

Though you can always find a few "history buffs" who love learning dates, events, and personalities of the past, most of us relate better to the common experience of the historical doldrums. History may be interesting to a few and boring to most, but is it *relevant* to anybody? Perhaps modern American or even European history has some important information to give us perspective, but what about *ancient* history? Or *church* history?

Many of you may be wondering about this right now. Why should Bible-believing Christians care about the early church? After all, if we have the inerrant Word of God at our fingertips, is there any reason we need to know the history of the church? Don't we have enough trouble making the Bible relevant to our postmodern world? Why complicate things with *history*?

Let me give you three reasons why believers should know the basics about the early church: a theological reason, an evangelistic reason, and a practical reason.

First, let's consider a *theological* reason. Jesus promised the disciples that when the Spirit comes "He will guide you into all the truth" (John 16:13). Although the ministries of the original apostles and prophets ceased in the first century, gifted pastors and teachers continued to contend for the faith. In Ephesians 4:11–12 Paul stated that the Spirit has gifted certain people to be not only apostles and prophets but also evangelists, pastors, and teachers—"for the equipping of the saints for the work of service, to the building up of the body of Christ." Did the Spirit continue to provide gifted pastors and teachers in the years following the apostles and prophets, or was their light extinguished by false prophets, politics, and persecution? Did the Spirit lead the church into all truth, or did the church instantly spiral into error and immorality as soon as the apostles died? Because we believe the Bible, we should be eager to learn from the pastors and teachers of church history—not only from more modern leaders such as Martin Luther, John Calvin, and Jonathan Edwards but also from those who learned their Bible and theology directly from the apostles and prophets themselves.

Second, let's reflect on an *evangelistic* reason. In recent years the soil of historical skepticism in the universities has become the seedbed for a campaign of criticism targeting the average "Dick and Jane." Intriguing theories of "competing Christianities," "lost Scriptures," and "Catholic conspiracies" have made their way from the universities into magazines, books, documentaries, and movies. Long-debated theories on the origins of Christianity have moved from the courtroom of academia to the uncontrollable circus of mass media. People with little background on the early church and no ability to discern between fact, fiction, and opinion sometimes buy into the most outlandish theories. Today, if we want to continue to share the credibility of Christ with "Dick and Jane," we as believers must know how to respond to historical criticisms.

- Did the church cover up Jesus's marriage to Mary Magdalene?

- Did second-century bishops change the Bible to support their theology?

- Did early Christians transform the humble carpenter from Nazareth into a mythical God-man in order to win converts?

- Did a few power-hungry churchmen defame and destroy those who disagreed with them?

From radical groups like the Jesus Seminar to works of fiction like *The Da Vinci Code*, attacks on Christianity and the Bible have never been more appealing to popular audiences. To effectively engage a culture of criticism with the gospel of truth, believers must know something about the *real* early church.

Third, let's focus on a *practical* reason. Hebrews 11 describes a great "cloud of witnesses surrounding us" (Hebrews 12:1)—men and women of the Old Testament who lived and died for their faith. These are not stories of mythical legends but living heroes inspired to great feats by the same Spirit who moves and empowers believers of every era. And just as Paul said, Old Testament history was written "for our instruction" (1 Corinthians 10:11). So, the history of the believers who went before us serves as instruction for us today. Indeed, the Old Testament saints had plenty of flaws and so do the heroes of the early church. Sometimes the opinions of the church fathers need to be corrected by God's Word. Other times we need to listen more attentively to what they have to say to us. In fact, in many ways the early church's premodern, pre-Christian world resembles our own postmodern, post-Christian world—both are hostile to the "narrow" claim that Jesus Christ is the only way to God. How the early church responded can serve as an example to us as we seek to shine our light in the dimming twilight of a world not favorable toward the claims of Christ.

Are you still yawning? If so, now is the time to wake up, take note of the heroic leaders of the early church, and listen to what they have to say to us today. In spite of all their imperfections and errors, those faithful men and women lived in a pluralistic and hostile culture not unlike our own and, therefore, serve as an example of how we can "contend earnestly for the faith which was once for all handed down to the saints" (Jude 3).

After the Apostles . . . Who?

Back in my Bible college days a well-meaning teacher once told us to turn our Bibles to Acts 29. Several of us snickered; some groaned. Of course, the book of Acts ends at chapter 28 with Paul in Rome waiting to testify before Caesar. The teacher responded, "Now it's *your* turn to act."

Bible-believing Christians often view the church that way. Even though Christ promised that the gates of Hades would not overpower the church (Matthew 16:18) and Paul said that the Spirit would continue to gift pastors and teachers to build it up (Ephesians 4:11–16), believers rarely think much beyond the book of Acts. But the acts of the Holy Spirit didn't end with the Acts of the Apostles. What happened in the years between the martyrdoms of Peter and Paul in the AD 60s and the finalization of the New Testament four hundred years later?

From Apostles and Prophets to Pastors and Teachers

By around AD 90—about sixty years after Christ's resurrection and the birth of the church—Christianity had grown significantly from its humble beginnings in Jerusalem. As you can see in the map on the next page, churches planted by the apostles now thrived in cities of Judea, Syria, Asia Minor, Macedonia, Greece, and Italy. From the larger cities, the churches continued to expand into smaller towns and then into more remote regions as well.

When the memories of the original founding apostles such as Peter, Paul, and James had begun to fade, the responsibility for these churches fell into the hands of the second and sometimes the third generations of leadership. Just as Paul had instructed Timothy, "The things which you have heard from me in the presence of many witnesses, entrust these to faithful men, who will be able to teach others also" (2 Timothy 2:2), so most of these "faithful men" had been selected by the apostles them-selves—or by their delegates, like Timothy and Titus. They had been trained in the Old Testament Scriptures, given whatever gospels or

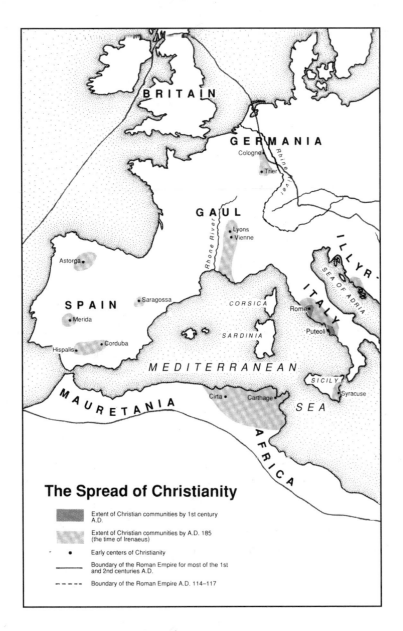

The Spread of Christianity

Extent of Christian communities by 1st century A.D.

Extent of Christian communities by A.D. 185 (the time of Irenaeus)

•   Early centers of Christianity

Boundary of the Roman Empire for most of the 1st and 2nd centuries A.D.

Boundary of the Roman Empire A.D. 114–117

Michael W. Holmes, *The Apostolic Fathers: Greek Texts and English Translations* (Grand Rapids, MI: Baker Books, 1992, 1999), 612–613. Used by permission of Baker Academic, a division of Baker Publishing Group.

writings of the apostles were available at the time, and ordained with the authority of the pastoral and teaching offices of the church. They were charged with defending the faith against all opposition, and they were warned that such opposition would come like a wildfire, as if fueled by the flames of hell itself.

But near the end of the first century there was still one place believers could go if they wanted to sit at the feet of an actual eyewitness of Jesus: Ephesus. At this time the apostle John lived and taught in western Asia Minor. During his years in Ephesus, John continued to receive visitors from churches throughout the world. One of these young men, Polycarp, was appointed by John to be the bishop of Smyrna.[1] Another bishop, Ignatius of Antioch, may also have known John personally. And we know that Papias of Hierapolis also sat at the feet of the aging apostle. It's no wonder that by the second century, after John finally passed on, Asia Minor—and particularly Ephesus—had become a center of Christianity in the Roman world. Though you could no longer visit with the apostle John himself, you could probably find his personal disciples in almost every city.

Early Heroes of the Faith

These early church leaders were not "celebrities" in the modern sense. They were more like "heroes" of the faith who stood strong against heresy and often died cruel deaths for their beliefs. Those who earnestly contend for the faith today stand in a long line of saints who have fought for the central truths of Christianity against false teachers and bloodthirsty tyrants. While most modern Christians know of the martyrdoms of the apostles, many are unaware of the martyrs who followed them—those who battled heresy, confronted paganism, and challenged the policies of persecution while often under the threat of brutal execution. Let's take a closer look at some of these second-century heroes whose writings survive to this day. You can compare the relative span of their lives in the chart on page 10.

Clement of Rome (martyred c. AD 100). This early pastor of Rome served at a time when the teachings of the apostles Peter and Paul were still ringing in the ears of the early Christians. In fact, some early church historians identify this Clement with the companion of Paul mentioned in Philippians 4:3. After writing a letter to the church in Corinth exhorting them to unity, Clement was martyred under the great persecution of Domitian.

Ignatius of Antioch (martyred c. AD 110). While under arrest and on his way to martyrdom in Rome, Ignatius wrote letters to various churches, including Ephesus, Smyrna, and Rome. He challenged the false teachings of Judaizers and Docetists who denied the true incarnation of Christ. He called for unity within the church in regard to the true doctrine of Christ and the essentials of the gospel.

Aristides of Athens (died c. AD 140). One of the earliest Christian apologists or "defenders" of the Christian faith, Aristides wrote an argument defending Christianity as superior to all other philosophies and religions, which he addressed to the pagan Emperor Hadrian around AD 125. His apology was widely read and later used by apologists such as Justin Martyr.

Polycarp of Smyrna (martyred c. AD 155). A friend of Ignatius and personal student of the apostle John, Polycarp served most of his life as

Church Leaders with Approximate Dates of Birth and Death

Primary Region of Ministry	People (approximate dates)
Syria	Ignatius of Antioch (c. 35–110); Theophilus of Antioch (c. 115–190)
Asia Minor	The apostle John (died c. 95); Polycarp of Smyrna (c. 65–155); Papias of Hierapolis (c. 70–155); Melito of Sardis (c. 110–190)
Greece	Aristides of Athens (c. 80–140); Athenagoras of Athens (c. 120–190)
Rome	Clement of Rome (c. 35–100); Justin Martyr (c. 110–165)
Gaul	Irenaeus of Lyons (c. 120–200)
Multiple Regions	Peter (died c. 67); Paul (died c. 67)
Year (AD)	40 50 60 70 80 90 100 110 120 130 140 150 160 170 180 190 200

the pastor of the church at Smyrna. He battled heretics like Marcion and advanced the gospel of Christ greatly, eventually suffering a heroic martyrdom in his eighties.

Papias of Hierapolis (died c. AD 155). A famous Christian who, as a young man, learned under the elderly apostle John and sought out the testimony of the other living disciples of Jesus, Papias also relayed information to later church fathers regarding the writing of the gospels and other New Testament books.

Justin Martyr (martyred c. AD 165). After vainly seeking truth in Greek philosophy, Justin converted to Christianity. He wrote several treatises against paganism, Judaism, and false Christian teachers and ultimately gave his life for his faith while teaching in Rome.

Melito of Sardis (died c. AD 190). A famous pastor and apologist of Sardis in Asia Minor, Melito reportedly wrote multiple works expounding on the incarnation and passion of Jesus Christ as well as defending Christianity against the claims of paganism, Judaism, and Christian heresies.

Athenagoras of Athens (died c. AD 190). Originally a philosopher of Athens, Athenagoras probably became a Christian after reading the works of the apostles in an attempt to refute them. Athenagoras was among those great apologists of the early church who presented a written plea for toleration of Christians to the Emperors Marcus Aurelius and Commodus around AD 177.

Theophilus of Antioch (died c. AD 190). The pastor of Antioch several decades after Ignatius, Theophilus is known for three letters he wrote to an unbeliever defending the basics of the Christian faith against common philosophical and historical objections. Although the doctrine of the Trinity previously existed, Theophilus was the first to use the specific Greek word for *triad* to refer to the Father, Son, and Holy Spirit.

Irenaeus of Lyons (martyred c. AD 200). Originally from Asia Minor, Irenaeus was a disciple of Polycarp who served as the pastor for the church in Lyons (modern-day France). There he wrote a massive, five-volume work, *Against All Heresies*, in which he demonstrated the true Christian faith and refuted the errors of the heretical groups of his day, especially the Gnostics.

Early Heroines of the Faith

When was the last time you heard a discussion about a woman's role in society, government, or the church? How about the role of women in ministry? Or in the family? Perhaps you've heard historians talk about male dominance and the oppression of women throughout history . . . or heard that it's about time for a woman president. Without a doubt, feminism — both in the world and the church — has become a major social and political force in the modern world. And given this cultural climate, we should not be surprised at the great interest in the position of women in the Bible and the early church.

In fact, a Christian woman once asked me this question about the early church: "All the church fathers you talk about were men . . . weren't there any *female* church fathers?"

I politely answered, "No, as far as we know, all the church fathers were male."

Church historians disagree on the status of women in the earliest centuries of the church. Some feminist scholars point out alleged oppression, rejection, and degradation of women in the Bible and other Christian writings. Others attempt to show that some women served in exalted positions—even positions equal to the apostles. The alleged conflict between men and women in early Christianity forms a major theme in the best-selling novel *The Da Vinci Code*. And some historians scour certain Gnostic writings for evidence of a conflict between female-dominated versions of Christianity and the male-dominated Catholic church.

In reality, male leadership was the norm in the early Roman world. There were exceptions, of course, but for the most part men led the way. The same was true in the churches of the New Testament as well as local churches that came after the time of the apostles. Though we have evidence that at least some early churches had both male deacons and female deaconesses, the bishops and presbyters were always men.

However, we should point out that although the primary leadership of the early churches was male, women were always *active, influential,* and *respected* in Christian churches (Romans 16:1–4). They taught, worshiped, and served beside men (Acts 18:25–26; 1 Corinthians 16:19). They were regarded as spiritual equals, just as Jews and Gentiles, slaves and free, were regarded as having equal standing before God (Galatians 3:28). In fact, the records of Christian martyrdom from the second century were filled with accounts of the heroic suffering of godly women for the sake of Jesus Christ. One example demonstrates the great respect afforded these true heroines of the faith. The martyrdom of Blandina, a well-respected

Christian woman, occurred during a vicious persecution of the Christians of Gaul (modern-day France) around AD 177. Blandina suffered day after day through numerous tortures as the governor tried to make her and other believers deny Christ. The survivors of that gruesome persecution recalled the ultimate testimony of Blandina with these words:

> But the blessed Blandina, last of all, having, as a noble mother, encouraged her children and sent them before her victorious to the King, endured herself all their conflicts and hastened after them, glad and rejoicing in her departure as if called to a marriage supper, rather than cast to wild beasts. And, after the scourging, after the wild beasts, after the roasting seat, she was finally enclosed in a net, and thrown before a bull. And having been tossed about by the animal, but feeling none of the things which were happening to her, on account of her hope and firm hold upon what had been entrusted to her, and her communion with Christ, she also was sacrificed. And the heathen themselves confessed that never among them had a woman endured so many and such terrible tortures.[2]

From the first testimony of the women at the tomb on Resurrection day (John 20:1–2) to the great testimony of the women who heroically gave their lives for the faith, women played an indispensable role in the spiritual and physical health of the early church . . . and they continue to do so today. Revisionist historians and popular fiction such as *The Da Vinci Code* would lead us to believe women were disrespected, ignored, or oppressed by brutish church fathers. Yet when we compare the role of women in the New Testament and the early church to the view of women in Judaism or

Paganism at the time, we see that women were both highly respected and greatly valued in the Christian churches.

Handing Down the Teaching of the Apostles

We don't have to scratch our heads and wonder what occurred after Acts 28 or speculate about what kind of believers came after the apostles. Today we all have access to the writings of many second- and third-generation believers, known as the apostolic fathers, apologists, or early church fathers. We can see that Paul's solemn charge in 2 Timothy 2:2 was indeed fulfilled when we explore for ourselves the writings of "faithful men" such as Clement, Ignatius, Polycarp, Papias, and Aristides, who were "able to teach others also"—Justin, Melito, Athenagoras, Theophilus, and Irenaeus.

2 Timothy 2:2 — Passing on the Tradition				
"The things which you have heard from me . . ."	". . . entrust these to faithful men . . ."		". . . who will be able to teach others also."	
FIRST GENERATION	SECOND GENERATION		THIRD GENERATION	
Peter		Clement		Justin
John		Ignatius		Melito
Paul	→	Aristides	→	Athenagoras
Luke		Polycarp		Theophilus
Timothy		Papias		Irenaeus

Without God working through the radical faith of these early Christians, the New Testament writings would have been lost like ashes in the wind, and the fundamentals of the faith would have suffocated under a smothering heap of heresy. Yet by God's providence, such a natural fate was not allowed. These early heroes of the faith kept the torchlight of the gospel burning through some of the most difficult periods of persecution and false teaching the church has ever known. Many of these great men and women fueled the flames by giving their own lives heroically for the faith.

As we study what the early Christians who came after the apostles believed, taught, and lived, we may find ourselves drawn to the things *we're* interested in. We are often intrigued that most of the earliest saints believed in a literal, future reign of Christ here on earth. Or we get hung up on the way they organized their churches with a bishop (pastor), presbyters (elders), and deacons. Or we point out that the church of the first couple of centuries baptized only believers and preferred immersion. However, we sometimes forget that the early fathers were primarily concerned with how to preserve and pass on the most central doctrines of the Christian faith in the face of persecution and false teaching. Therefore, we'll focus on three overlapping areas that were of utmost importance to the early fathers.

1. The Savior: Jesus Christ, Our Lord

2. The Source: Authentic Scripture

3. The Center: Orthodox Tradition

If we can grasp what the early church believed about these three areas—Christ, Scripture, and orthodoxy—we'll not only have a good understanding of the early church itself but also be equipped to correct the misrepresentations and distortions of today's critics and skeptics.

A few years ago an unbelieving employer of mine called me into his office to discuss *The Da Vinci Code*, which had just been published. Knowing I was a seminary student, he asked me several specific questions about claims made by the book: Was Jesus married? Did Constantine change the Bible and cover up the true Jesus? Though I hadn't read the novel, I had studied the early church enough to answer his questions and to refute the fiction with real facts. And since that time, I've been called on to respond to other believers and unbelievers with similar questions and concerns.

When coworkers, employers, family members, or friends ask you these questions, do you know enough about the early church to respond? If not, read on.

The Savior: Jesus Christ, Our Lord

Several years ago I taught a course on the doctrine of Christ for laypeople at Dallas Theological Seminary's Center for Biblical Studies. I'll never forget what happened to me the first night. Because my class consisted of mature believers from solid, evangelical churches, I decided to rush through the doctrine of the preexistence and eternality of Christ, assuming that the class would be quite familiar with these basic doctrines. As soon as I finished pointing to some biblical texts about Christ's eternal existence before creation, one gentleman in the front row dropped his Bible on the floor and loudly announced: "Okay, I'm going to just admit it. I've never heard this before. I thought Jesus started out in the manger. You mean He always existed? Why haven't I heard this before tonight?" That evening I learned I couldn't assume that everybody had a solid foundation concerning the person of Jesus Christ—even those who had spent years in Bible-believing churches!

Since that time, my teaching experience has confirmed this over and over again. Today many believers have the whole Bible in their hands and still have a poor understanding of Jesus Christ. By contrast, believers in the early church *did* have a firm grasp on the doctrine of Christ's person and work *even before* they had a complete collection of the New Testament books. In fact, Jesus Christ stood at the very center of everything they believed, confessed, and practiced.

The Deity and Humanity of Jesus Christ

Works of fiction like *The Da Vinci Code* and heretical sects like the Jehovah's Witnesses suggest that the doctrine of the divinity of Christ, which states that Jesus is not only fully man but also fully God, developed slowly throughout church history. They often point to the political motives of Emperor Constantine and the alleged speculations of the Council of Nicaea around AD 325 as the watershed events in history when the human Jesus of Nazareth was officially exchanged for the divine Son of God.

The New Testament and the teaching of the early church both demonstrate clearly that Christians have always believed Jesus to be both God *and* man. In John 1:1, 14, we see that the eternal Son of God (the "Word") was called "God," and at the moment of His miraculous conception, He took on full humanity—including a body of material flesh. Repeatedly in the New Testament, Jesus is declared both man and God (John 1:1, 14; Romans 1:3; Galatians 4:4; Colossians 2:9; Philippians 2:6–8; and 1 Timothy 3:16). The idea that later Christians selected or changed Scripture to downplay Christ's humanity in favor of divinity is complete fiction. In fact, Christians in the first and second centuries had to *defend* Christ's full humanity against heretics like some Gnostics who argued that Christ was *only* God and not really human (1 John 4:2; 2 John 1:7).

On the heels of the apostolic period, Ignatius of Antioch wrote to the church in Ephesus, "There is only one physician, who is both flesh and spirit, born and unborn, God in man, true life in death, both from Mary and from God, first subject to suffering and then beyond it, Jesus Christ our Lord." [3]

Around the middle of the second century Melito of Sardis preached, "For he was born a son, and led as a lamb, and slaughtered as a sheep, and buried as a man, and rose from the dead as God, being God by his nature and a man." [4]

Today some critics have claimed that the idea of Jesus as God and man developed late in the first century, perhaps in the AD 90s, and took some time to catch on. And *The Da Vinci Code* suggested Constantine invented the deity of Christ four hundred years after Jesus lived. However, the consistent testimony of the early church is clear: Jesus is both God and man, one with — but distinct from — the Father and the Spirit.

The Work of Jesus Christ

The early fathers maintained that salvation was not obtainable by works done in human power but only by grace through faith because of the work of the Father, Son, and Holy Spirit. At the center of this was the work of Jesus Christ, the God-man, who died for our sins and rose from the dead. To the early Christians, it was inconceivable that a person could be saved and deny the central truths of the person and work of Jesus Christ. Although they rarely speculated on exactly *how* Christ's death atoned for their sins, one thing was sure: apart from Jesus Christ, there was no salvation.

Clement of Rome, a contemporary of the apostle John, summed up the center of salvation through Jesus Christ:

> And so we, having been called through his [God the Father's] will in Christ Jesus, are not justified through ourselves or through our own wisdom or understanding or piety or works which we have done in holiness of heart, but through faith, by which the almighty God has justified all who have existed from the beginning; to whom be the glory for ever and ever. Amen.[5]

Just a few years later, Ignatius emphasized the vital relationship between the Father, Son, and Holy Spirit in salvation, "You are stones of a temple, prepared beforehand for the building of God the Father, hoisted up to the heights by the crane of Jesus Christ, which is the cross, using as a rope the Holy Spirit."[6] For the early Christians, salvation was wrought by the harmonious working of the Father, Son, and Holy Spirit.

Some say that the early church taught salvation by works or the doctrine of "baptismal regeneration"   that is, the idea that water baptism is necessary for salvation. It *is* true that the early fathers placed a greater emphasis on the changed life and outward manifestation of salvation through love and good works than some evangelicals do today. However, these good works were the expected result of *saving faith*. Those who claimed to have faith without good works were regarded as deceiving themselves and others. Baptism was closely linked to conversion, but this linkage is clear in the New Testament as well. People in the New Testament and in the early church responded to the gospel not by coming forward during an invitation, by praying a "sinner's prayer," or by raising their hand with their eyes closed and head bowed—but by confessing their faith before others and submitting to water baptism. There was such a close, sometimes immediate, chronological relationship between belief, repentance, confession, conversion, and baptism that these terms were often used interchangeably, and it was inconceivable that a person would be considered a "Christian" without being baptized. This is quite different than saying that the literal water of baptism actually saves. Baptism was viewed as a *biblical response* to the preaching of the gospel.

Yet one must always remember that for most teachers in the early church, salvation did not center on baptism, good works, church membership, or some other human standard but on the person and work of Jesus Christ. They believed these other things naturally followed a genuine conversion, and converts who confessed Christ but lacked a Christian lifestyle were suspect. Nevertheless, Jesus Christ's death and resurrection formed the center of salvation. Apart from Him there could be no eternal life.

The Source: Authentic Scripture

When I was a brand-new believer at age seventeen, a girl from school learned of my interest in spiritual things and invited me to her church. I eagerly accepted. When she saw that I brought my Bible with me, she commented, "You can leave that in the car. You won't need it."

I frowned and brought my Bible anyway. A minute later a hundred people stared at me: the invader with the Bible. You see, there were only two

Bibles in the sanctuary that day: one belonged to me; the other belonged to the church elders, the "apostles," who sat like judges at a table at the front of the church. I later learned that the church had twelve "apostles" who read and interpreted the Bible for the church.

Needless to say, I never visited that church again.

That strange sect and the early church had at least one thing in common: the average church member didn't have his or her own Bible. But there was also a major difference: *the early church had no other choice.* Hand-copying the Bible was time-consuming, and most of the earliest churches had only a partial New Testament. Although the Roman Catholic Church of the Middle Ages has become notorious for its biblically illiterate membership and priesthood, the early Christians knew the Bible well even without their own personal copies. But to read and study the Scriptures they had to come together often . . . sometimes daily.

Imagine living at a time like that, when you had to share the Scriptures with your church. Even then, the Scriptures you shared may have included only the Old Testament, the gospel of Matthew, a handful of letters from Paul, and a letter from Peter. To hear these writings, you had to gather together with others and listen as the pastor or elders read them aloud.

Once in a while a visiting Christian from a distant region might stop by with another letter from one of the apostles. Eventually somebody might bring another gospel. But unless you knew the person who brought the writing, how would you know it was authentic? How would you know it hadn't been changed? After all, several false teachers were writing letters and fake gospels, claiming that they were written by apostles. And one man—the son of a pastor, no less—was cutting out parts of the gospels and letters of Paul he didn't agree with and passing the remainder off as the inspired version of the Christian Scriptures.

Welcome to the church of the second century.

Because of the serious task of protecting, preserving, and passing on the truth about Jesus Christ, the early churches did everything they could to make sure the Scriptures they had—both the Old and New Testaments—were the authentic, inspired, and inerrant Word of God. No "Bible Wannabes" were allowed, and if they found any, they rejected them instantly. Writings from other pastors and teachers like Ignatius or Polycarp were welcomed as well, but they were not granted the same level of authority as the letters of the apostles and prophets. The early church wanted the whole Bible and nothing more, and because of their insight, wisdom, and patient endurance, we're able to have confidence in our Bible today.

The Canon: How the Early Church Identified the New Testament

One summer when touring the Mormon temple in Salt Lake City, Utah, I was appalled at the artwork portraying Jesus and Paul with such people as Joseph Smith and Brigham Young. But I was even more aghast when my tour guide quoted the Book of Mormon in the same breath as the gospel of Matthew. On what basis could they add these writings to the Old and New Testaments?

This brings up some important questions. How do we know the Bible is complete? Are we missing some books? Who decided that what we have in the New Testament exhausts God's written revelation? How do we know that the books we have are the right ones?

There are many different views about how the ancient writings actually became part of our Bible. Some have said that, for political and theological reasons, a council of bishops voted on these particular books out of hundreds of competing writings. Others say the church ran each book through a rigorous test to determine whether it was inspired. The issue of the "canonicity" of the books of the Bible is an important topic. (The Greek word *canon* means "rule" or "standard.") Sorting out fact from fiction in this matter will help strengthen our confidence that the Bible we hold in our hands contains only the books that are meant to be there—and none that don't belong.

Because Christians accepted the same Old Testament canon as the Jews, the early church debated very little about which books should be included. So for the very earliest Christians, "Scripture" consisted of the Old Testament books as we have them in our Bibles today. However, during the first sixty years of the church (until about AD 100), important documents were still being written by Spirit-led apostles and prophets. Because these inspired writings were not all written by the same person, at the same time, in the same place, the consolidation of these various writings into what we call the *New Testament* understandably took some time.

How did this occur? In the same way you and I can tell whether a letter we receive is from a close friend or from a total stranger, the Christian leaders and communities to whom the apostles and prophets originally wrote knew which books were *authentic* (written by a true apostle or prophet), *true* (the information was reliable), and therefore *authoritative* (the apostles had been given divine authority to lead the church, so their inspired words were commands from God). Almost immediately these apostolic writings were copied and passed around to other churches. Very soon, churches began to use these "New Testament" writings in teaching and worship. So for most of the New Testament books, there was little question about whether or not they were authoritative for the faith and practice of the churches.

But wouldn't the second- and third-generation Christians in those churches lack certainty about those writings? No, the Christian communities that originally received and copied the letters would have known that their writings were authentic and whether or not changes had been made to them.

Let me give you a more modern illustration. In Dallas, Texas, there's a Bible church called Scofield Memorial Church—named after one of its earliest pastors, C. I. Scofield, editor of the famous Scofield Reference Bible. In that church's archives I have read documents from the earliest pastors, including handwritten notes from C. I. Scofield. How do I know these documents are authentic? Well, I learned of them from an elderly woman who had been at the church for decades who had learned about them from another member of the church who had been around at the time of C. I. Scofield. Therefore, I personally received authentication and can vouch that they're genuine. The same thing is true about New Testament writings in the early church. For the majority of apostolic writings, their authenticity was never in question.

For example, in AD 95 the apostle John may have handed his gospel over to Onesimus, pastor of the church in Ephesus, who then sent copies to Polycarp in Smyrna, who handed it down to Irenaeus, and so on. For most books, therefore, there would have been no question about their authenticity—at least in the region in which they had been written.

Eventually remote Christians in other churches and regions would come to accept these writings as well, as they researched each document's history and examined its content.

Even when we hear about "disputed" books that took longer for all the churches to accept, we should actually be *encouraged* by this news rather than discouraged. Why? Because this prudence indicates that the early church leaders were extremely cautious regarding which writings they accepted, and they did the research and investigation necessary to establish whether or not the tradition authenticating a particular writing was true. Once they were able to research the origin and contents of the books, the early church leaders reached a consensus of which writings to accept as authoritative. Although the majority of our New Testament books were collected and used together by about AD 200, the final affirmation of our present New Testament canon occurred at the Council of Carthage in AD 397. The Council of Carthage did *not* vote on these books from among dozens of competing "nominations" or potential "candidates" for Scripture but simply acknowledged the writings that Christians all over the world had already accepted by that time—and have received ever since.

When a Mormon missionary once asked me how I knew there could be no additions to the New Testament canon, my answer was simple: because the disciples of the apostles themselves as well as the early church regarded the collection of inspired writings to be complete. When the apostles and prophets passed away, the inspiration of inerrant Scripture ceased. This has been the view of the majority of Christians from the very beginning.

What, then, can we say about the so-called "lost books" like the Gnostic Nag Hammadi writings? These are all later books often written by heretical sects or false teachers—usually forgeries that were deceptively attributed to apostles or prophets who were long dead by the time the false books were written. Even many non-Christian scholars admit that the New Testament books we have in the Bible are the earliest and most authentic Christian writings available, and all scholars concede that the so-called "lost Scriptures" are all later, inauthentic writings that most often present doctrines at odds with the biblical view of Jesus. The strange—even bizarre—stories contained in these writings certainly fall under the category of "cleverly devised tales," as Peter called them in 2 Peter 1:16. If you were to pick up a copy of these "lost writings," you'd instantly recognize that the accounts are decorated with far-fetched myths and legends.

From the Prophet's Pen to the Layperson's Lap

The inspired writings of the apostles and prophets in your Bible came through a process of *inspiration, transmission,* and *translation.* Charles Ryrie defined inspiration this way, "God superintended the human authors of the Bible so that they composed and recorded without error His message to mankind in the words of their original writings."[7]

Around AD 95 Clement of Rome wrote, "You have searched the Scriptures, which are true, which were given by the Holy Spirit; you know that nothing unrighteous or counterfeit is written in them."[8] Clement obviously shared the same high view of Scripture as evangelicals today.

Because the material they used for paper in the ancient world deteriorated with time and use, original documents did not last as long as they do today. To preserve a written document, a person had to copy it by hand, thus the stage of *transmission*. Those who copied Scripture were usually well-educated men of God who were extremely meticulous in their craft. Although minor errors in spelling and word placement may have crept into copies of these documents here and there, when we compare the thousands of copies available, we can determine what the original writing said.

Finally, because the Old Testament was written in Hebrew or Aramaic and the New Testament was written in Greek, these books have been translated over the centuries into numerous languages so that people all over the world can understand them. Though most of them are based on the same documents, the various translations of the Bible we have today differ from one another to some degree due to the philosophy of translation (literal or paraphrase) or to the scholars' positions regarding the definitions and translations of words. However, major modern translations, including the New American Standard Bible, faithfully render the original meaning and notify readers of alternate translations.

Because of the faithfulness of the early churches in identifying and preserving true Scripture, we can be confident that the Bible we hold in our hands contains the whole truth . . . and nothing more.

Definitions of Ancient Writings

Canonical Writings	These writings of the Old and New Testaments were accepted by Jesus, the apostles, and the early Christians as inspired by the Spirit. They were written by apostles or prophets without doctrinal or factual error. Christians believe the last books of the New Testament were written by the AD 90s.
Apocrypha and Pseudepigrapha	These writings were not universally regarded as canonical. Some of these claimed to have been written by famous Old and New Testament personalities but were later determined to be forgeries (*pseudepigrapha* means "false writings"). Occasionally, early Christians accepted a few of these writings as authentic — especially if they contained passages that supported their theology. But in the process of "canonization" — affirming the truly inspired writings — apocryphal and psuedepigraphic writings were eventually rejected.
Early Church Fathers	These writings are by pastors and teachers after the New Testament period. They acknowledged that their writings did not carry the same authority as the canonical books. These writings often defended, explained, or applied some aspect of canonical books or the orthodox faith. The term "Apostolic Fathers" refers to the early church fathers that are believed to have lived closest to the time of the apostles. While most of the writings of the early church fathers present the central teachings of orthodox Christianity, several may represent "fringe" elements that eventually led to heretical groups.
Dead Sea Scrolls	The Dead Sea Scrolls contain no New Testament texts but are a collection of writings discovered in 1948 in caves of the Qumran region near the Dead Sea in Israel. Most scholars believe they were composed or copied between 200 BC and AD 100. They contain important Hebrew manuscripts of Old Testament books and informative historical documents produced by the Qumran community — a Jewish separatist sect that followed a strict moral code and expected the end of the world to come soon.

Continued on next page

Definitions of Ancient Writings, *continued*

Nag Hammadi Library	These writings are mostly Gnostic pseudepigraphic writings forged between the second and fourth centuries to advance heretical views about God and Christ. The thirteen volumes of numerous writings were discovered in Nag Hammadi, Egypt, in 1945 and have been the subject of intense study ever since. However, prior to this time, historians were aware of such ancient Gnostic documents through the references and quotations of similar heretical writings mentioned in the works of the early church fathers.

The Center: Orthodox Tradition

What do you think of when you hear the word *orthodox*? For some it conjures up images of icons and idols, incense, altars, and priests in funny hats rattling off an ancient liturgy in Greek or Russian. Other Christians associate the term *orthodoxy* with their own beliefs, often broadening the definition to include all issues of theology rather than focusing only on what is most essential. Anybody who disagrees with any aspect of their views is considered a "heretic." The results of this type of "orthodoxy" have been graceless dogmatism and mean-spirited debates over every area of disagreement.

The accurate definition of *orthodox* is "a correct opinion" about something. However, *traditional orthodoxy has always been limited to the essential truths of the Christian faith*—things that deal with the person of God, Jesus Christ, and salvation. To err in matters of orthodoxy means to err in matters of salvation. Eternal life is at stake. Heresy would then be viewed as "damnable doctrine"—opinions held by those who could not possibly be true

Christians. Because they had a firm grasp on the person and work of Jesus Christ and placed their doctrine of Jesus at the center of their theology, early Christians also had a stable center of orthodoxy—unyielding in the essentials but quite diverse in secondary matters.

Orthodoxy vs. Heresy

In the twentieth century the distinction between orthodoxy and heresy began to come under attack. Some scholars have suggested that early Christianity was characterized not only by radical diversity and conflict between Christians but what became known as orthodoxy was at one time just one of many versions of Christianity.[9] These modern-day skeptics teach that the orthodox group eventually suppressed all opposition and selected only the New Testament books that agreed with their theology. In the process, the skeptics claim, the orthodox church suppressed the rich diversity of early Christianity and rewrote history to support its views—a classic example of "only the strong survive," "winner take all," and "the winner writes the history."

It's important to recognize that these scholars *presuppose* that the resurrection of Christ is false; therefore, they can't believe that there is one true form of Christian teaching. They are also often driven by modern-day agendas that emphasize religious pluralism, tolerance, and even immoral lifestyles. Their claims—though dressed in the garb of intellectualism and Ivy League respectability—are not based on the clear facts of history but upon biased presuppositions common in our day.

So when you hear scholars talk about "lost Christianities," "radical diversity" in the early church, "lost Scriptures," or "proto-orthodoxy," you must understand that they are actually denying the truth of orthodoxy.

In fact, they regard certain forms of "suppressed" heresy to have been more true to the historical Jesus and His teachings than the biblical orthodoxy taught by the early church.

Unity and Orthodoxy Model

If Jesus rose from the dead, then secondary heresies sprouted from an original, early apostolic orthodoxy while the fathers continued to refine its explanation and defense of Jesus Christ's person and work.

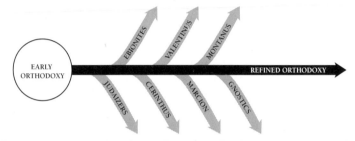

Diversity and Conflict Model

If Jesus did not rise from the dead, then the version of theology now called "orthodoxy" was a secondary development that arose from an original diversity of views about Jesus of Nazareth's person and work.

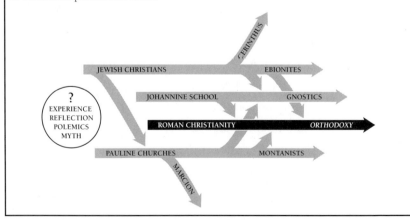

The Center of Orthodox Theology

Early in American history a Bible teacher decided that all the competing denominations displeased God and defamed the gospel. So he set out to unite all the believers in one church based only on the Bible. If the Bible didn't say it, they wouldn't do it. Well, his attempt at reconstructing the original church based on Scripture failed. The result was not one single church but just another denomination listed in the phone book, and even his new church has split several times into smaller branches.

Christianity today is certainly diverse! In fact, some of the differences between denominations have been the cause of much disagreement, debate, and even conflict throughout the centuries. However, it's sometimes easy to miss all of the important things churches have in common when we focus on all of the minor things over which we disagree. All true Christian churches, denominations, and teachers are now and have always been in agreement over the most central doctrines of the faith.

True Christians, from the earliest days of the church to the present, have held to these core biblical doctrines:

- the infallibility of Scripture as the final authority in faith and practice

- one eternal, triune God in three persons: Father, Son, and Holy Spirit

- the absolute deity and perfect humanity of Jesus Christ, His virgin birth, sinless life, substitutionary death, bodily resurrection, and literal future return

- the special creation and fall of humanity

- salvation by grace through faith

- the eternal life of believers and condemnation of unbelievers

Those who have strayed far from this center of orthodoxy have been regarded as outside the true Christian faith.

Before the New Testament writings were collected and regarded by all believers as canonical, how did early Christians preserve the truth? How did they guard the central beliefs from change while protecting believers from heresy? One way was through confessions and creeds that summarized the basic doctrines of the faith as handed down by the apostles. Another way was through the central authority of the pastors and teachers of the church who had received their theology directly from the apostles and prophets. Worship in the community provided another method—including reading Old and New Testament Scriptures, songs and hymns, and rituals rich with theology like baptism and the Eucharist or Lord's Supper.[10]

Creeds and Councils in the Early Church

In the early church—perhaps as early as the days of the apostles themselves—believers used creeds (or "confessions") to fulfill a dual purpose. First, creeds helped to summarize and define the cardinal doctrines of Christianity for those being instructed in the faith prior to or following baptism. The creedal formulas provided unity among all Christians, despite differences on minor issues. Second, because certain phrases in the various confessions were designed to rule out false teachings, creeds helped the church keep false doctrine from gaining ground in the assemblies. For example, the Ebionites taught that Jesus was not born of a virgin but was instead the natural son of Joseph, and Gnostics taught that a lesser deity—not the almighty Father—created the material universe.

Some of the earliest confessions are found in the New Testament itself: John 1:1–5; 1 Corinthians 15:3–5; Philippians 2:5–11; Colossians 1:13–20; and 1 Timothy 3:16. The early church carried on this practice of utilizing short summaries of the faith. Throughout the second century we see examples of these creeds. For instance, Irenaeus of Lyons wrote:

> The Church, though dispersed throughout the whole world, even to the ends of the earth, has received from the apostles and their disciples this faith: . . . in one God, the Father Almighty, Maker of heaven, and earth, and the sea, and all things that are in them; and in one Christ Jesus, the Son of God, who became incarnate for our salvation; and in the Holy Spirit, who proclaimed through the prophets the dispensations of God, and the advents, and the birth from a virgin, and the passion, and the resurrection from the dead, and the ascension into heaven in the flesh of the beloved Christ Jesus, our Lord, and His [future] manifestation from heaven in the glory of the Father.[11]

As the church continued to encounter false teachers and new questions, the creeds developed and grew. The doctrines concerning the Father, Son, and Holy Spirit continued to play the central role with the person and work of Christ always in the spotlight. The Nicene Creed (approved at the Council of Nicaea in AD 325) and the Constantinopolitan Creed (approved in AD 381) combated the errors of Arius, who denied the true deity of Christ. The Council of Ephesus (held in AD 431) condemned the teaching of Nestorius, who divided Christ into two separate persons—one divine, the other human. The Council of Chalcedon (held in AD 451) condemned the teaching that the divine nature and the human nature of Christ were mixed and blurred into a new nature, which was neither wholly human nor wholly divine. In all of these creeds and councils the ancient doctrine of the incarnation was affirmed and defended—Jesus Christ is one person with two complete natures, human and divine, without mixture and without separation.

To this day, these creeds and councils continue to hold a place of prominence in Christian history, theology, and worship. Though not all churches and denominations pay close attention to these creeds, all true Christians agree with the basic theology expressed in them. In fact, if someone asked you to summarize the main points of the Christian faith, chances are you would use patterns very similar to the creeds and confessions of the early church.

The True Catholic Church

When I was in grade school, a teacher was talking about the different religions and churches of the world. She explained that most people in their country were Christians, then asked the class, "How many of you consider yourselves to be Christians?"

All the students raised their hands . . . except one girl. She looked around the room, spotted one of her friends raising her hand, and shouted, "Hey, Tina, put your hand down! We're not Christians, we're Catholics!"

Are *you* a catholic? The Apostles' Creed declares, "I believe in . . . the holy catholic church." Though most evangelicals probably couldn't agree on exactly what it means to be "evangelical," they'll probably agree that evangelicals are *not* catholic. However, by the ancient definition of that term, evangelicals are actually *more* catholic than the medieval and modern Roman Catholic Church!

The term *catholic* comes from the Greek word *katholikos*, which means "universal" or "general" as opposed to local and specific. Ignatius of Antioch was the first to use this term in reference to orthodox Christian churches. In an exhortation to avoid heretics who were trying to woo people away from the true gospel of Jesus Christ and the correct understanding of Scripture, Ignatius instructed the local church in Smyrna to submit to the teaching of their bishop, Polycarp, who had been a personal student of the apostle John. Ignatius wrote, "Wherever the bishop appears, there let the congregation be; just as wherever Jesus Christ is, there is the catholic church." [12] In this context *catholic* refers to the body of Christ throughout the world under the headship of Jesus Christ, just as the local church in Smyrna was under the headship of their pastor, Polycarp.

Later in the second century the term *catholic* was used to distinguish between orthodox churches that preserved apostolic doctrine and heretical churches that were founded by false teachers. It also came to emphasize churches that were united around the same Scriptures and common confessions, though they may have been separated by language, geography, and even diverse traditions. So evangelical churches—whether Lutheran, Presbyterian, Baptist, Methodist, Episcopalian, Independent, or something else—are, in fact, "catholic" in the original sense of the word.

On the other hand, the Roman Catholic Church is actually *not* catholic by this standard but seems to represent the renegade tradition of a single, local church—the church in Rome.

The early church survived the onslaught of heresy by banding together in close-knit, local churches under ordained pastors and teachers centered on the person and work of Jesus Christ. These catholic churches met frequently for prayer, accountability, Scripture reading, worship, and teaching. By faithful membership in the orthodox catholic churches, believers would be safe from false teaching. Those who rebelled against the pastors and teachers, however, ran the risk of falling prey to heresy. By unity and submission to the true teaching of the bishop, orthodoxy was preserved and heresy defeated.

The Historic Heresies

Ahhhhh . . . the weekend's here at last. You have a couple hours on a Saturday afternoon to do nothing. No work, no thinking, no fretting . . . just rest. You drop into your recliner, put your feet up, close your eyes and . . .

Knock, knock, knock! You spring up from your seat, swing open the front door, and find yourself face-to-face with a pair of Jehovah's Witnesses. Within seconds you go from resting on the recliner to wrestling with heretics. They use the same Old and New Testament books as you (with some major modifications), but they deny that Jesus is God. In fact, they even try to paint a false picture of an early church that changed from a belief in Jesus as simply the first created being to Jesus as a divine member of the Trinity. When do they claim this change supposedly occurred? About the time of Constantine in AD 325.

Heresies like these are not new. False teachers have been ruining people's Saturdays for centuries. Jesus and the apostles predicted the coming of false prophets and teachers whose intent was to deceive unprepared Christians and rob unbelievers of the truth (Matthew 24:11; 2 Peter 2:1). Although they differed from one another in many ways, each of these heretics rejected the central truths of the Christian faith. Consider a few of these ancient heretics:

Docetists (c. AD 90–200). The Greek word *dokeō* means "to seem," and the Docetists taught that Jesus Christ only *seemed* to be a man, but He was in reality only a spiritual being. These heretics either taught a heresy like Cerinthus—separating the physical man Jesus and the spiritual being Christ into two persons—or a heresy like Marcion—who suggested that the body of Jesus Christ was just a temporary phenomenon but not really material or fleshly. Today, some still view the physical world as evil and the spiritual or mental world as good—a philosophy of creation that lies at the root of ancient docetism.

Gnostics (c. AD 100–400). Various Gnostic heretics in the second century included Basilides, Saturninus, and Valentinus. They taught that Christ was only one of many spirit beings that sprang forth from God to bring salvation by special knowledge (*gnosis*) to the spiritually elite. They wrote their own scriptures to support their views including the writings contained in the Nag Hammadi Library.

Ebionites (c. AD 100–300). These were Judaizing Christians who emphasized the observance of the law and denied the virgin birth and deity of Christ. Ebionites should be distinguished from Nazarenes or Jewish Christians in the early church who followed Jewish customs but remained orthodox in their theology and continued to fellowship with other catholic churches.

Marcion (c. AD 150). The rebellious son of the pastor of Sinope, Marcion was a wealthy merchant who had been expelled officially from his home church for heresy. He rejected the Old Testament God as a lesser, inferior being who created the imperfect universe. Marcion also gathered his own New Testament canon of mostly Pauline letters after editing them to fit his theology. He infiltrated the church at Rome, where he gave a gift equivalent to perhaps $250,000 in today's currency. A few years later, when the church in Rome realized he was teaching heresy, they excommunicated Marcion and refunded his entire gift. Marcion then set out to start his own Marcionite churches that continued to exist for several centuries.

Arius (c. AD 320). Although Arius lived almost two centuries after Marcion, his particular heresy was so extreme that it required a meeting of pastors worldwide to officially denounce it. Arius denied the true deity of Christ and taught that the Son was not an eternal being, but had a beginning; therefore, Jesus must have been a created being. After promoting this heresy with delightful ditties that caught the attention of the common people, Arius's teachings were condemned at the Council of Nicaea.

Orthodoxy vs. Ancient and Modern Heresies

Teaching	Beliefs and Practices	Modern Forms
Orthodoxy (AD 100–Present)	Orthodoxy affirmed the doctrine of the Trinity (one divine nature in three persons, Father, Son and Holy Spirit) and the incarnation (two natures, human and divine, in one person, Jesus Christ, without division, separation, confusion, or mixture).	Orthodoxy includes all true Christians today who affirm one God in three persons (Father, Son, and Holy Spirit) with each member of the Trinity being fully God, co-eternal and co-equal, but distinct in function and role.
Ebionites (AD 100–300)	The Ebionites denied the deity of Christ, embracing Jesus as simply a great moral teacher.	Some believe in only a human, "historical Jesus," denying the deity of Christ. Groups such as the Jesus Seminar and unbelieving historians fall into this category.
Docetists, Gnostics, Marcionites (AD 100–400)	These groups denied the humanity of Christ, embracing Christ as a purely spiritual being uncontaminated by a physical body of flesh.	Today, examples of this heresy include mystical, New Age philosophies and religions who teach that the physical world is evil and only the spiritual world is good. Christians today who focus entirely on spiritual salvation in heaven rather than the resurrection of the body fall prey to Docetic tendencies. Extreme charismatic groups actually reflect Gnostic practices that seek to receive "special revelations" from God.

Continued on next page

Orthodoxy vs. Ancient and Modern Heresies, *continued*

Teaching	Beliefs and Practices	Modern Forms
Sabellians, Modalists (AD 200–300)	These groups denied the distinction between Father, Son, and Spirit and taught that the three are one person with different names.	Those who subscribe to this teaching today are often called "Oneness" Pentecostals, modalists, Unitarians, and include all others who teach that the Father, Son, and Spirit are all the same person with three different names.
Arians (AD 300–400)	Arians denied the full deity of Christ, teaching that Jesus was the first and greatest creature made by God but that He is not co-eternal and co-equal with the Father.	Jehovah's Witnesses believe that Jesus is equal to the archangel Michael, which is very similar to the original Arian heresy.
Apollinarians (AD 350–400)	The Apollinarians denied the full humanity of Christ, believing that the fully divine Son replaced the human spirit in the man, Jesus.	Some Christians who misunderstand the incarnation believe the Son of God replaced the spirit of the man, Jesus, resulting in a humanity that is incomplete.
Nestorians (AD 400–500)	The Nestorians denied the true union between the deity and the humanity of Christ.	Some Christians misunderstand the union of God and man, suggesting that throughout the life of Christ, sometimes the human person acted and sometimes the divine person acted.

The Early Church . . . Why?

On May 19, 2006, the film adaptation of Dan Brown's *The Da Vinci Code* hit theaters. While some Christian leaders responded with calm refutations of its outrageous claims, others panicked. I've heard of young people, already unstable in the Christian faith, who read *The Da Vinci Code* and abandoned the church. I also know of unbelievers who completely fell for the fictional theories of early church conspiracies and cover-ups. Indeed, *The Da Vinci Code* found a sympathetic audience in an already skeptical culture.

However, the truth is that fictional works like *The Da Vinci Code* are fragile, dry twigs on a much larger tree of historical criticisms attacking the Christian faith. Even after those little branches are broken off or ignored, the tree itself continues to grow in the church's backyard. A number of outspoken, unbelieving scholars are touting as "truth" a version of history that clouds with doubt the faith "once for all handed down to the saints" (Jude 3).

Maybe you've heard their names or seen their faces: the Jesus Seminar, John Dominic Crossan, Bart Ehrman, Elaine Pagels, Karen King, John Shelby Spong. They've been interviewed for PBS, *20/20*, *Time*, and *Newsweek*, parading as experts of church history. They use intriguing phrases like "lost Christianities," "lost Scriptures," "suppressed Gnostic gospels," "oppressed women of the early church," and "diversity and conflict in early Christianity." They scoff at conservative Christians for believing that Jesus Christ literally rose from the dead and founded an orthodox church. They mock evangelicals for teaching Scripture as the inspired Word of

God. They advance an agenda of liberalism, feminism, and pluralism, teaching that there are many ways to God.

Without doubt, the critics' tree poses a more serious menace to the household of faith than *The Da Vinci Code* ever will. Its roots ripple the sidewalks leading to our church's front doors, shift the foundations upon which our historical doctrines rest, and block the light that helps people see the truth. These critical scholars try to make the fundamentals of the Christian faith look silly, rolling their eyes at claims that Jesus is the only way to salvation. And they do all this by appealing to "recently discovered documents" like the Gnostic Nag Hammadi Library, the Dead Sea Scrolls, and other "historical facts" they claim disprove the biblical version of Christian origins. As a result, evangelism, Bible teaching, and godly living can be frustrated.

The reality is that most Christians today aren't equipped to handle the challenges of these critics. Most don't know how to answer the skeptic on their TV screens. But this doesn't mean it can't be done. A few evangelical scholars have responded to these larger historical issues in books that even theological beginners can understand. However, too many people are writing books against Dan Brown rather than Bart Ehrman—cracking fragile twigs rather than addressing the root problems.

In response to this gap in believers' awareness of their own faith, I have painted a picture of the early church in broad strokes. Now names like Ignatius, Polycarp, and Irenaeus shouldn't frighten you away. Instead, you should be drawn to their testimonies as defenders and martyrs of the faith. You should now understand that the person and work of Jesus Christ has stood at the center of orthodox theology from the time of the apostles through the present day. Though the church's explanations and defenses of orthodoxy have continued to grow and develop through the centuries, the basic understanding of Jesus Christ as fully God and fully man, who died for our sins and rose from the dead, has marked the distinction between orthodoxy and heresy from the beginning.

If this book has whetted your appetite for learning more about the heritage of the early church, I would recommend any of the resources on the following pages to help you continue to add more structure to the basic sketch drawn here. As you continue to explore the world in which the Bible took shape and to investigate the priceless legacy of the early catholic church, I pray that you will continue to grow in your confidence in Scripture, in the central truths of Christianity, and in your faith in our great God and Savior, Jesus Christ.

Resources for Probing Further

This short book introduces several key issues of the early church that would take a lifetime of study to explore. The following resources will help you dig deeper into these important topics. Most of these books should be available from your church library, public library, bookstore, or online bookseller, though some may be out of print. Although I cannot endorse everything a writer asserts, these are some of the best resources for their particular areas of study.

To help you decide which resources are best for you, they have been labeled as "beginner," "intermediate," "advanced," or "expert."

1. The Savior: Jesus Christ, Our Lord

Erickson, Millard J. *The Word Became Flesh: A Contemporary Incarnational Christology.* Grand Rapids: Baker Books, 1991. (advanced)

Grillmeier, Aloys. *Christ in Christian Tradition.* Vol. 1, *From the Apostolic Age to Chalcedon (451).* 2d rev. ed., trans. John Bowden. Atlanta: John Knox, 1975. (expert)

Habermas, Gary R. and Michael R. Licona. *The Case for the Resurrection of Jesus.* Grand Rapids: Kregel, 2004. (intermediate)

Harris, Murray J. *Three Crucial Questions about Jesus.* Grand Rapids: Baker Books, 1994. (intermediate)

Hurtado, Larry W. *Lord Jesus Christ: Devotion to Jesus in Earliest Christianity.* Grand Rapids: Wm. B. Eerdmans, 2003. (advanced/expert)

Jones, Peter. *Stolen Identity: The Conspiracy to Reinvent Jesus.* Colorado Springs: Victor, 2006. (intermediate)

Komoszewski, J. Ed, M. James Sawyer, and Daniel B. Wallace. *Reinventing Jesus: What The Da Vinci Code and Other Novel Speculations Don't Tell You.* Grand Rapids: Kregel, 2006. (intermediate)

Strobel, Lee. *The Case for Christ: A Journalist's Personal Investigation of the Evidence for Jesus.* Grand Rapids: Zondervan, 1998. (beginner)

Wright, N. T. *The Resurrection of the Son of God.* Christian Origins and the Question of God. Minneapolis: Fortress, 2003. (expert)

2. The Source: Authentic Scripture

Beckwith, Roger T. *The Old Testament Canon of the New Testament Church and Its Background in Early Judaism.* Grand Rapids: Wm. B. Eerdmans, 1986. (intermediate)

Bruce, F. F. *The Canon of Scripture.* Downers Grove, Ill.: InterVarsity, 1988. (intermediate)

Geisler, Norman, ed. *Inerrancy.* Grand Rapids: Zondervan, 1980. (intermediate)

Lutzer, Erwin W. *Seven Reasons Why You Can Trust the Bible.* Chicago: Moody, 1998. (beginner)

Metzger, Bruce M. *The Canon of the New Testament: Its Origin, Development, and Significance.* Oxford: Clarendon, 1987. (advanced/expert)

3. The Center: Orthodox Tradition

Bock, Darrell L. *The Missing Gospels: Unearthing the Truth behind Alternative Christianities*. Nashville: Nelson Books, 2006. (intermediate)

Frend, W. H. C. *The Rise of Christianity*. Minneapolis: Fortress, 1984. (advanced)

Guy, Laurie. *Introducing Early Christianity: A Topical Survey of Its Life, Beliefs and Practices*. Downers Grove, Ill.: InterVarsity, 2004. (intermediate/advanced)

Patzia, Arthur G. The *Emergence of the Church: Context, Growth, Leadership and Worship*. Downers Grove, Ill.: InterVarsity, 2001. (intermediate)

Skarsaune, Oskar. *In the Shadow of the Temple: Jewish Influences on Early Christianity*. Downers Grove, Ill.: InterVarsity, 2002. (intermediate/advanced)

Swindoll, Charles R. and Insight for Living. *The Way of Truth in a World of Fiction: Beyond* The Da Vinci Code *Workbook*. Plano, Tex.: IFL Publishing House, 2006. (beginner/intermediate)

Turner, H. E. W. *The Pattern of Christian Truth: A Study in the Relations between Orthodoxy and Heresy in the Early Church*. London: Mowbray, 1954. (expert)

4. Writings of Heroes and Heretics in the Early Church

Robinson, James M., ed. *The Nag Hammadi Library in English*. Trans. Coptic Gnostic Library Project. 1st U.S. ed. New York: Harper and Row, 1977. (advanced/expert)

Schneemelcher, Wilhelm, ed. *New Testament Apocrypha*. Rev. ed. Ed. and trans. R. McL. Wilson. 2 vols. Louisville: Westminster/John Knox, 1991–1992. (advanced/expert)

Stewart-Sykes, Alistair. *Melito of Sardis, On Pascha, with the Fragments of Melito and Other Material Related to the Quartodecimans*. Crestwood, N.Y.: St. Vladimir's Seminary Press, 2001. (intermediate/advanced)

The Apostolic Fathers: Greek Texts and English Translations. Updated ed. Ed. and rev. Michael W. Holmes, ed. and trans. J. B. Lightfoot and J. R. Harmer. Grand Rapids: Baker Books, 1999. (NOTE: English-only edition is also available.) (intermediate/advanced)

The Ante-Nicene Fathers: Translations of the Writings of the Fathers down to A.D. 325. Ed. Alexander Roberts, James Donaldson, and A. Cleveland Coxe. Vol. 1, *The Apostolic Fathers, Justin Martyr, Irenaeus*. American reprint ed. New York: Charles Scribner's Sons, 1899. (intermediate/advanced)

Christian Classics Ethereal Library. This is an online collection of historical Christian writings in the public domain. Access is free, and their collection is quite extensive. These can be accessed at www.ccel.org. (intermediate/advanced)

Glossary of New or Unique Terms in the Early Church

Apocrypha: A group of writings that were never universally and officially regarded by Christians as part of the biblical **canon**.

Apologists: Church **fathers** who defended **orthodox** Christian faith and practices against pagan rulers, philosophers, and **heretics**.

Apostles: A reference to disciples of Jesus who were personally chosen as eyewitnesses of His resurrection to carry the good news around the world. After John died in the AD 90s, the apostles were replaced by **bishops** and teachers in local churches.

Apostles' Creed: An early **creed** that emphasized the work of the Father, Son, and Holy Spirit. Though it was not written by the **apostles**, it reflected the basic **orthodox** teachings of the apostles.

Apostolic Fathers: The earliest of the church **fathers** who lived in the period from about AD 50 to 150 and who likely knew some of the original **apostles** or prophets of the New Testament church.

Arianism: This fourth-century **heresy** denied the full deity of Christ. Arians taught that Jesus was the first and greatest creature made by God before creation but not the true God, co-eternal and co-equal with the Father. Arianism was condemned by the **Council of Nicaea**.

Bishop: In the period after the **apostles**, this term referred to the pastor, shepherd, or leading **presbyter** in a local church. In the **early church**, bishops presided only over churches in their own cities.

Canon: The books of the Old and New Testaments that have been accepted by the Christian church as inspired by God and are therefore authoritative.

Catholic: A term that means "universal" or "general" as opposed to local and specific. In the **early church**, this referred to the global, **orthodox** church, different from the later Roman Catholic Church.

Council of Carthage: In AD 397, a council of Christian leaders who affirmed the New Testament **canon** of twenty-seven books exactly as we have it today.

Council of Chalcedon: In AD 451, a council of Christian leaders who condemned the teaching that the divine nature and the human nature of Christ were mixed and blurred into a new nature, neither wholly human nor wholly divine.

Council of Nicaea: In AD 325, a council of Christian leaders who affirmed the full deity and humanity of Christ and condemned the **heresy** of **Arianism**.

Creed: A short summary statement used to instruct believers about the basics of **orthodox** Christianity, often preceding baptism of a new believer. Creeds tended to remain consistent in essential content but varied in language and form from church to church.

Deacons: Local church leaders who served the practical and administrative needs of the church under the authority of the **bishop** and **presbyters**.

Docetism: From the Greek word *dokēo* meaning "to seem." This early **heresy** claimed the Son of God only seemed to be a man, but He was not truly united with physical humanity in a real body of flesh.

Early Church: The term *early church* often refers to the people and events from the end of the **apostles'** time (about AD 100) to the church councils (about AD 300), when the beliefs and practices of the churches most resembled the New Testament churches. Perhaps the most foundational and formative period of the early church was the century from AD 100 to 200.

Ebionism: A **heresy** that taught that Jesus was simply a great moral teacher — denying the full deity of Christ.

Fathers: The **bishops**, **presbyters**, and other teachers of the **early church** who, through teaching and writing, defended the **orthodox** faith against **heresy**.

Eucharist: A Greek word meaning "thanksgiving." This often simply referred to the "thanksgiving meal" of the Lord's Supper or Communion and the prayer of thanks offered to God when the **early church** observed this practice.

Gnostics: From the Greek word *gnosis* meaning "knowledge." A variety of **heresies** that emphasized special knowledge received from a secret God different from a less powerful creator god. Gnostics believed this secret God revealed the true nature of the universe to a spiritual elite, and this knowledge led to liberation from the evil, material world. Many Gnostics also taught **docetism**.

Heresy: A separatist teaching that caused people to turn away from the essential **orthodox** teachings of the church and follow false teachers. Their beliefs are called *heresies*, and their teachers are often called *heretics*.

Judaizers: These early **heretics** believed Christians must also observe the Jewish laws. Some of these were guilty of **Ebionism**.

Marcionites: The followers of Marcion in the middle of the second century rejected the Old Testament God, removed many books from the New Testament, and taught **docetism**.

Nag Hammadi Library: A collection of books discovered in 1945 containing mostly **Gnostic** writings and **pseudepigrapha** written in Coptic (ancient Egyptian). None of these are authentic writings of **apostles**, and none were ever universally accepted as part of the biblical **canon** by **orthodox** Christians.

Orthodox: A Greek word meaning "correct opinion." Orthodox believers have always held to the essential, unchanging truths of the Christian faith. These truths include the doctrines of the Trinity, the person and work of Jesus Christ, and other foundational biblical beliefs.

Presbyters: In the **early church**, presbyters (or "elders") were the pastors and teachers who led local churches in cooperation with the presiding **bishop** and the assistance of the **deacons**.

Pseudepigrapha: Forged documents written deceptively in the names of famous Old and New Testament people. Occasionally, early Christians thought a few of these writings might be authentic, but eventually the whole church rejected them as false. Most of the **Nag Hammadi** writings and **Apocrypha** are pseudepigraphic.

Scribes: Well-educated men of God who meticulously preserved Scripture through copying. Because the materials they used for paper in the ancient world deteriorated with time and use, original documents did not last, and they needed to be copied repeatedly by scribes.

Tradition: A term used by the **early church** to describe the essential **orthodox** beliefs and practices handed down from generation to generation through Scripture, **creeds**, and instruction by **bishops** and **presbyters** in the **early church**. Protestants believe that through the centuries the original tradition of the **apostles** was perverted by human additions and that the earliest tradition can be seen in the New Testament and the writings of the **apostolic fathers, apologists**, and other **fathers** of the **early church**.

We Are Here for You

If you desire to find out more about knowing God and His plan for you in the Bible, contact us. Insight for Living provides staff pastors and women's counselors who are available for free written correspondence or phone consultation. These seminary-trained and seasoned men and women have years of pastoral experience and are well-qualified guides for your spiritual journey.

Please feel welcome to contact our Pastoral Ministries department by calling the Insight for Living Care Line: 972-473-5097, 8 A.M. through 5 P.M. Central Time. Or you may write to the following address:

> Insight for Living
> Pastoral Ministries Department
> Post Office Box 269000
> Plano, Texas 75026-9000

Endnotes

1. The word translated *bishop* is the Greek *episkopos*, which means "overseer." Originally it referred to the pastor or shepherd of a local church who, with the elders or presbyters, served as the leaders ordained to preach and teach. The bishop in the early church was similar to the pastor of the local church today.

2. Eusebius, *Ecclesiastical History* 5.1.55–56. In *The Nicene and Post-Nicene Fathers*, ed. Philip Schaff and Henry Wace, 2nd series, vol. 1, *Eusebius: Church History, Life of Constantine the Great, and Oration in Praise of Constantine*, American reprint ed. (Christian Literature, 1890; reprint, Peabody, Mass.: Hendrickson, 1994), 217.

3. Ignatius, *Letter to the Ephesians* 7.2. In *The Apostolic Fathers: Greek Texts and English Translations*, updated ed., ed. and rev. Michael W. Holmes, ed. and trans. J. B. Lightfoot and J. R. Harmer (Grand Rapids: Baker Books, 1999), 141.

4. Melito, *On Pascha* 8. In Alistair Stewart-Sykes, *Melito of Sardis, On Pascha, with the Fragments of Melito and Other Material Related to the Quartodecimans* (Crestwood, N.Y.: St. Vladimir's Seminary Press, 2001), 39.

5. 1 Clement 32.4. In *The Apostolic Fathers: Greek Texts and English Translations*, 63–65.

6. Ignatius, *Letter to the Ephesians* 9.1. In *The Apostolic Fathers: Greek Texts and English Translations*, 143.

7. Charles C. Ryrie, *Basic Theology* (Wheaton, Ill.: SP Publications, Victor Books, 1986), 71.

8. 1 Clement 45.2–3. In *The Apostolic Fathers: Greek Texts and English Translations*, 79.

9. Some examples of authors and scholars include Bart Ehrman, Elaine Pagels, Karen King, John Shelby Spong, John Dominic Crossan, and Robert Funk.

10. The term *eucharist* comes from the Greek word meaning "thanksgiving," *eucharistia*, and refers to the giving of thanks for Jesus Christ's saving work celebrated with the bread and wine.

11. Irenaeus, *Against Heresies* 1.10.1. In *The Ante-Nicene Fathers: Translations of the Writings of the Fathers down to AD 325*, ed. Alexander Roberts, James Donaldson, and A. Cleveland Cox, vol. 1, *The Apostolic Fathers, Justin Martyr, Irenaeus*, American reprint ed. (New York: Charles Scribner's Sons, 1899), 330.

12. Ignatius, *Letter to the Smyrnaeans* 8.2. In *The Apostolic Fathers: Greek Texts and English Translations*, 189–191.